100
THINGS TO DO IN
SAN DIEGO
BEFORE YOU
DIE

100
THINGS TO DO IN
SAN DIEGO
BEFORE YOU
DIE

● ●

MARIA DESIDERATA MONTANA

Library of Congress Control Number: 2015954884

ISBN: 9781681060224

Design by Jill Halpin

Cover Image: Maria Desiderata Montana

Printed in the United States of America
16 17 18 19 20   5 4 3 2 1

Please note that websites, phone numbers, addresses, and company names are subject to change or cancellation. We did our best to relay the most accurate information available, but due to circumstances beyond our control, please do not hold us liable for misinformation. When exploring new destinations, please do your homework before you go.

DEDICATION

To my husband, John, and my two children, Lucia and Frank. You have always been and forever will be my inspiration!

CONTENTS

• •

• •

• •

PREFACE

Although I cannot claim San Diego as my birthplace, I am fortunate to call it home. Like many residents in the local area, I am a transplant who couldn't ignore the calling of America's Finest City. For more than two decades, I have lived and played in one of the most temperate climate areas of the continental United States, where locals rarely plan their day around inclement weather. In fact, the year-round moderate temperatures make this area a perfect destination for those who crave outdoor activities. Within a short driving distance, you can be relaxing on a sandy ocean beach, hiking through miles of forest trails, skiing on wintry mountain slopes, strolling through endless rows of grapevines, or marveling at the wonders of a starry desert evening. San Diego is also home to top-tier educational institutions that drive world-class science and innovation and thrives from a strong military presence.

The hardest part about writing *100 Things To Do In San Diego Before You Die* was narrowing the list from an avalanche of possibilities. This book represents my best attempt to highlight the must-see opportunities in our fair city. Although I included many of the obvious outdoor attractions that have made San Diego famous, I also focused on other aspects of the area that must be experienced, including our deeply historic and cultural charms, natural wonders, melting pot of culinary offerings, and endless calendar of social events. So whether you're a local or local wanna-be, please enjoy my vision of the ultimate bucket list!

- -

100

THINGS TO DO IN
SAN DIEGO
BEFORE YOU
DIE

© Maria Desiderata Montana

FOOD AND DRINK

DINE PENTHOUSE STYLE
AT MISTER A'S

For fifty years, Mister A's has been a landmark dining destination. Located on the 12th floor of the 5th Avenue Financial Center building in Banker's Hill, guests can experience modern American food with French and Mediterranean influences at this stunning fine-dining penthouse restaurant located just minutes from downtown. The dining room is light and bright, with floor-to-ceiling windows boasting panoramic views of San Diego Bay, Balboa Park, Coronado, Point Loma, and even the world-famous San Diego Zoo. A heated outdoor patio allows for a perfect "dining al fresco" experience. Classic and timeless cocktail libations are never out of style here, and light and simple food preparations offer a refined elegance.

2550 5th Ave., #406, San Diego, 619-239-1377
bertrandatmisteras.com

Neighborhood: Banker's Hill

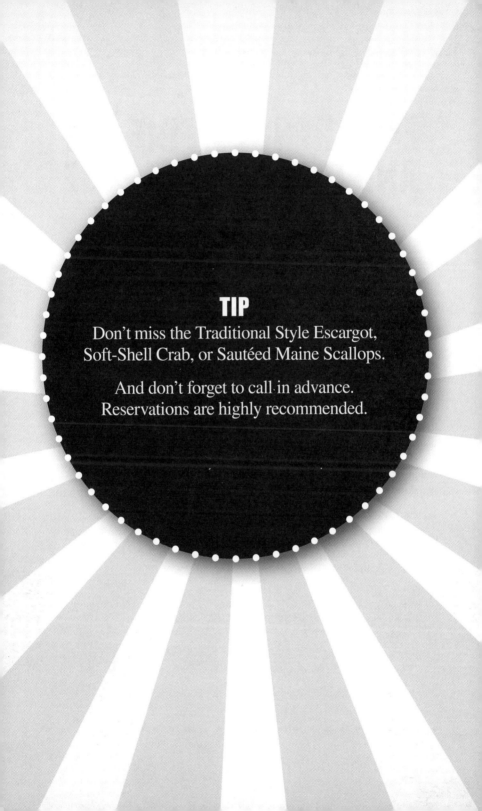

TIP

Don't miss the Traditional Style Escargot,
Soft-Shell Crab, or Sautéed Maine Scallops.

And don't forget to call in advance.
Reservations are highly recommended.

EXPERIENCE A FINE ART AND DINING ESCAPADE
AT A.R. VALENTIEN

Set inside The Lodge at Torrey Pines, A.R. Valentien takes its name from a talented early 1900s California artist whose works in ceramics, watercolors, and oils are now valued collector's items. The restaurant's decor also includes an exhibit of original Valentien artworks. You will certainly feel transported whiling away the hours in a charming dining room with its prominent view of the Torrey Pines Golf Course and Pacific Ocean just off the bluffs in the distance. Executive Chef Jeff Jackson oversees the culinary concept and menu development at this 169-room California Craftsman–Style property, which includes A.R. Valentien. A mastermind of a market-driven cuisine sourced from some of the finest local organic farms and fishmongers, Jackson ensures freshness and taste with every bite.

11480 N Torrey Pines Rd., La Jolla, 858-777-6635
arvalentien.com

Neighborhood: La Jolla

EAT DINNER
AT HIGH TIDE AT THE MARINE ROOM

Opened in 1941, The Marine Room has surprised celebrities, world figures, residents, and visitors with its customary seaside vista showcasing dramatic displays for guests to watch. Don't miss your chance to experience their popular high tide dinners, as plumes of surf cascade off panoramic windows. All tables, both windowside and elevated booths, offer almost touchable views of the incoming water. Relying on the bounty of the nearby farmers markets, fishermen, and ranchers, Executive Chef Bernard Guillas and Chef de Cuisine Ron Oliver bring an international influence to their cuisine, sharing their love and passion for cooking while showcasing their local heritage. From seafood favorites to the seasonal and exotic, the menu is an elegant and everlasting tale of two chefs.

2000 Spindrift Dr., La Jolla, 858-459-7222
marineroom.com

Neighborhood: La Jolla

EAT CUSTOM-MADE OYSTERS
AT IRONSIDE FISH & OYSTER BAR

The biggest showstopper at Ironside Fish & Oyster Bar is the exclusive "Ironside Select," a custom oyster that was created from seed to delicious briny bivalve with Minterbrook Oyster Company out of Puget Sound in Washington State. Ironside Selects are hand–farmed throughout the harvesting process. The oysters are then sorted, graded, and placed in special trays, which are then placed back into the saltwater for a period of time. This careful process minimizes the time out of the water prior to shipment and regenerates chips in the shells. It also helps to ensure that the oysters will arrive fresh and strong. You just might become an oyster aficionado after tasting the distinctive flavor profile of this special oyster that is mild and sweet, with a smooth finish and a touch of brine.

1654 India St., San Diego, 619-269-3033
ironsidefishandoyster.com

Neighborhood: Little Italy

GET HOOKED
ON A LEGENDARY FISH TACO

As a college student, Ralph Rubio made regular pilgrimages to surf the beaches of Mexico. After one day of satisfying his hunger at a seaside taqueria, he met his true love, the fish taco. With the help of his entire family, Ralph opened his first Rubio's, a walk-up stand in Mission Bay, San Diego in 1983. It didn't take long for the fish taco craze to take hold, leading to a large number of Rubio's locations based locally and spreading across five states in the Southwest. Using fresh and high-quality ingredients, the Original Fish Taco® is made with moist Alaskan pollock, a mild white fish that's beer-battered-by-hand, cooked until crisp, and topped with shredded cabbage, mild salsa, and Rubio's signature white sauce, all nestled inside a warm corn tortilla.

rubios.com

Neighborhood: all over San Diego

EAT AT
A FIVE-STAR RESTAURANT

Located inside the Fairmont Grand Del Mar, Addison is Southern California's only Forbes Five-Star and AAA Five Diamond restaurant. In 2010, Executive Chef William Bradley received the designation of Grand Chef from Relais & Châteaux, one of only 160 chefs on five continents to hold this title. Also a James Beard Award nominee, Bradley provides guests with a grand taste of his culinary talents amidst an ambiance of sophisticated elegance. Bradley is well known for taking an artisanal approach to his food preparation by combining local ingredients with contemporary French influences. The menu changes with the seasons and is offered as a multicourse experience, allowing you to pace yourself with every delicious bite. The cuisine is paired with an award-winning wine list of nearly thirty-six hundred selections.

5200 Grand Del Mar Way, San Diego, 858-314-1900
addisondelmar.com

Neighborhood: Carmel Valley

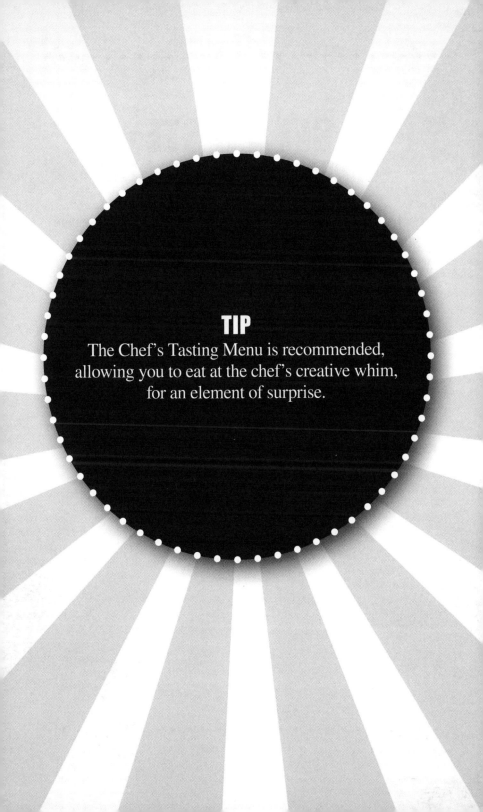

TIP

The Chef's Tasting Menu is recommended,
allowing you to eat at the chef's creative whim,
for an element of surprise.

GET A TASTE
OF CRAFT BEER AT ITS BEST

From humble beginnings, the Stone Brewing Co. is now the largest in Southern California and in the Top 10 in the United States. It all started with a great idea between two beer lovers and grew into one of the most talked about success stories in San Diego. Over the years, this brewery has created a great many different products but is almost always based on the unique high hop content that results in a distinctively bitter taste synonymous with Pale Ales. Be sure to visit one of the two locations for a guided tour through the working brewery, extensive gardens, and option to dine on an upscale meal in the bistro. It's a must-see for anyone who appreciates the transformation of a dream into reality.

1999 Citracado Parkway, Escondido, 760-294-7899
2816 Historic Decatur Rd., #116, San Diego, 619-269-2100
stoneworldbistro.com

Neighborhood: Escondido and Liberty Station

GRAB A TASTE
OF ASIA ON CONVOY STREET

Concentrated just a short drive north of downtown, the Convoy Corridor is a melting pot of Asian cuisines. You could easily spend a week tasting all the different styles for lunch and dinner. The Dumpling Inn is the best place to savor traditional Northern Chinese dumplings, including pork, fish, vegetable, and beef curry. At Sushi Dokoro Shirahama, you can choose from twenty-five to thirty different kinds of extraordinary Japanese sushi items, seasonal fishes, and sake. Manna Korean BBQ is fun for the whole family, with an unbelievable all-you-can-eat Korean BBQ dinner that allows guests to grill their choice of meats and vegetables. Many other establishments serving Thai, Vietnamese, and Filipino cuisines are also located within several blocks.

Neighborhood: Between Clairemont Mesa Blvd and Balboa Avenue

EAT A CLASSIC
GRANNY SMITH APPLE PIE

Eat a slice or two of a traditional apple pie like grandma used to make at the Julian Pie Company. Founded in 1986 by Liz Smothers, the Julian Pie Company first started when Smothers began peeling apples and baking pies at a local pie shop. As more and more people started tasting the pies, Smothers wanted to start her own business, and the Julian Pie Company was born. Her handmade apple pies are classic, with a golden and flaky crust, but the crumb-top pies are the most popular. The Julian Pie Company attracts countless locals as well as visitors from around the world and has been written about in many food and travel magazines, including a documentary featured on the Food Network cable channel.

2225 Main St., Julian, 760-765-2449
julianpie.com

Neighborhood: Julian

DINE ON A YACHT

Whether you're planning to celebrate a holiday or special occasion, this venue is the perfect choice for enjoying time with family or friends. A unique experience for visitors and residents alike, a luxury dinner cruise aboard one of the seven Hornblower yachts cruises San Diego Bay nightly. Begin your evening with a glass of champagne, followed by an extravagant three-course meal prepared by talented chefs, including such classics as filet mignon and shrimp scampi. Live entertainment will entice your senses as you float quietly beneath the Coronado bridge and marvel at the sparkling San Diego skyline. Since cruises last three hours, you have plenty of time to enjoy warm breezes on the deck or heart-pumping music in the dance room.

1800 North Harbor Drive, San Diego, 619-686-8700
hornblower.com

Neighborhood: Downtown

ENJOY AFTERNOON TEA
AT THE WESTGATE HOTEL

For that very special occasion, or just because, take your opportunity to relax in classic luxury while sipping tea, listening to the melodious sounds of a harp, and indulging in delectable tea sandwiches as well as a nice array of pastries, sugary scones, and fresh seasonal berries. Women are especially fond of the fancy dresses, hats, and gloves, as they idle the day reminiscing about the "good old days" where technology takes a backseat. It's particularly common for mothers and daughters to gain some quality family time. In addition to formal teas, champagne and wine are also available.

1055 2nd Ave., San Diego, 619-238-1818
westgatehotel.com

Neighborhood: Downtown

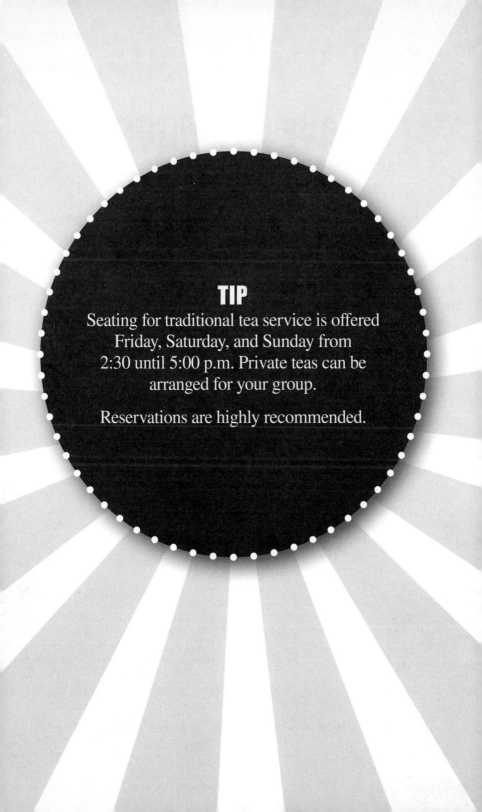

TIP

Seating for traditional tea service is offered Friday, Saturday, and Sunday from 2:30 until 5:00 p.m. Private teas can be arranged for your group.

Reservations are highly recommended.

HAVE A FAMOUS
FAST FOOD BURGER

A popular SoCal institution, don't give the big brush-off to this fast food chain that offers a good old-fashioned burger cooked to order. Nothing on the menu here is frozen, prepackaged, or overprocessed. Burger patties are made from fresh, 100% pure beef and are free of additives, fillers, and preservatives. All ingredients are delivered fresh daily, including hand-leafed lettuce, real American cheese, fresh onions, and juicy tomatoes. The buns are even freshly baked using old-fashioned, slow-rising sponge dough. And it doesn't stop there. The In-N-Out French fries come from potatoes shipped right from the farm, which are individually cut in-house and cooked in 100% pure vegetable oil. Even the shakes are made with real ice cream. What are you waiting for?

www.in-n-out.com

Neighborhood: all throughout San Diego

TAKE A TOUR
OF TEMECULA WINE COUNTRY

Whether it's a party bus, private limo, or other touring option, you have to make a day to be pampered with a guided ride through one of Southern California's most extensive vineyard regions. Less than an hour north of San Diego, the Temecula Wine Country boasts more than forty wineries producing fifty different varieties of wine. The diversity is directly linked to the natural microclimates of the area, allowing for successful crops of grape varieties ranging from cool-climate whites to Mediterranean-climate reds. Many wineries have tasting rooms and restaurants as well as some gift shops and even a number of hotels, spas, and B&Bs. With the many touring options available from San Diego, you can relax and enjoy all that Temecula has to offer.

Temecula Valley Winegrowers Association
29377 Rancho California Road, Suite 203, Temecula, 951-699-3626
temeculawines.org

Neighborhood: Temecula

STALK A CELEBRITY CHEF
AT JUNIPER AND IVY

The Juniper and Ivy kitchen is helmed by Celebrity Chef Richard Blais, winner of Bravo's Top Chef All-Stars and successful restaurateur, cookbook author, and television personality. Dining areas feature natural hickory-stained tabletops, elevated leather booth spaces and white lacquered tables, and an outdoor patio offers al fresco dining year-round. The daily, yet evolving menu is based on the chef's ever-changing inspiration and culinary vision, specifically highlighting the region's bountiful and fresh local produce and presenting guests with unexpected iterations on the classics. Divided into several categories, the menu includes snacks, raw, toast, and pasta in addition to plates, both small and large, as well as dessert. Additionally, a 4×4 four-course tasting menu, composed of four small bites and four small plates is available with an optional wine pairing.

2228 Kettner Blvd., San Diego, 619-269-9036
juniperandivy.com

Neighborhood: Outskirts of San Diego's Little Italy

EAT AT
THE FAMOUS SEARSUCKER

Television personality and celebrity Chef Brian Malarkey has several successful restaurants across the United States. Each one opened to rave reviews, namely Searsucker, which was named the country's #2 Hottest Restaurant. Serving what they call "New American Classics," this socially driven concept all began in San Diego's Gaslamp District and now has expanded to four locations, including Caesar's Palace in Las Vegas. Chef Malarkey focuses on making the dining experience more than just good food, with dining rooms arranged with large tables and plenty of couches to maximize interaction with fellow guests. Menu items include a number of twists on classic dishes but also highlight Malarkey's imaginative spirit, ranging from Habanero Coriander Pickles to a Pork Butt Roast with whiskey apples and bacon emulsion.

611 5th Ave., San Diego, 619-233-7327
www.searsucker.com

Neighborhood: Downtown San Diego and Carmel Valley

DISCOVER
FARM-TO-TABLE FARE

In 2006, three-time James Beard award nominee Carl Schroeder established San Diego's famed Market Restaurant + Bar with great success and a very loyal following. With a strong belief in organic and natural foods, Schroeder's passion for locally sourced ingredients and hyper-seasonal cuisine are on display for dinner every evening. He seeks out the best produce, seafood, and meat from local markets, and his passion for perfection and the spontaneous nature of what is available are showcased in the daily changing menu. Start your dining adventure with a craft cocktail accented with farm-fresh fruit or choose from an award-winning wine list. With menu favorites of Organic Baby Beet and Local Citrus Salad to Cast-Iron-Seared Yellowtail, this is a deliciously exclusive food-filled escapade you don't want to miss!

3702 Via De La Valle, Del Mar, 858-523-0007
marketdelmar.com

Neighborhood: Carmel Valley and Del Mar

DEVOUR DONUTS
BY THE SEA

Now in its third generation of family ownership, the VG Donut & Bakery has called Cardiff home since 1969. This locally famous icon serves some of the best bakery items in all of San Diego, but it's the wide range of classical donuts that keep long lines waiting nearly every morning any day of the week. Best of all, they are one block west of Highway 101 and the San Elijo State Beach, making access to the ocean just a simple walk. There's no better experience in the morning than a freshly made donut hot from the oven and waiting to pair with your favorite coffee drink. Be sure to take your prize down the street and enjoy on a bench overlooking the spectacular views. Just remember to pack plenty of napkins!

106 Aberdeen Dr., Cardiff, 760-753-2400
vgbakery.com

Neighborhood: Cardiff by the Sea

GET THE SWEETEST PICKS
AT THE CARLSBAD STRAWBERRY FIELDS

For more than fifty years, the Carlsbad Strawberry Company has been growing strawberries on a 40-acre field that borders the Batiquitos Lagoon to the east and Interstate 5 to the west at the Cannon Road location in Carlsbad, California. You may even see the man that walks the farm and cracks the bullwhip to keep away the birds that like to pick the seeds off the strawberries when he's not around. The strawberry harvest usually takes place between January and July, but the U-Pick is usually open to the public sometime in the spring. Since the temperate climate and large amounts of sunshine make for a supersweet strawberry, take your time while walking through the fields to look for the ripest ones. Remember, those buckets fill up fast!

1050 Cannon Rd., Carlsbad, 760-603-9608
carlsbadstrawberrycompany.com

Neighborhood: Carlsbad

TIP

Be sure to watch the website for
U-Pick announcements.

HAVE A WORLD-FAMOUS
MAI THAI

Nothing beats a famous cocktail paired with spectacular views of San Diego Bay and the downtown skyline. With more than two million sold, the world-famous Bali Hai Mai Tai is a juiceless and very strong concoction made of Coruba Jamaican Dark Rum and Ron Castillo Light Rum with a dash of Orange Liqueur and Trader Vic's Orgeat Syrup, and a splash of Sweet and Sour. Opened in 1955 by San Diego restaurateur Tom Ham on the then newly constructed Shelter Island, the Bali Hai restaurant was the island's first "tiki temple," named after the song popularized by the musical *South Pacific*. Two famous tiki icons: Mr. Bali Hai, a large wood sculpture at the front entrance, is still greeting guests, and "The Goof," a playful and mysterious remnant, is still standing guard on the roof of the restaurant.

2230 Shelter Island Dr., San Diego, 619222-1181
balihairestaurant.com

Neighborhood: Shelter Island

EAT YOUR WAY
THROUGH THE LIBERTY PUBLIC MARKET

Serving as a one-stop specialty shop as well as a daily farmers market, the Liberty Public Market is a twenty-two-thousand-square-foot artisan mecca located in Point Loma's Liberty Station. This $3 million mixed-use retail and commercial market is a place where you can pick from year-round fresh produce sourced from surrounding regional farms as well as locally procured seafood and old-fashioned butcher services. A unique lineup of merchants and vendors will offer everything from classic lobster rolls and New England clam chowder to delicious premium ice cream, homemade tortillas, artisanal breads and pastries, locally roasted coffee, fine wines, and much more. Besides offering fresh fare to take home, the market also offers quick-service counters, allowing guests to enjoy food on-site.

2816 Historic Decatur Rd., San Diego
libertypublicmarket.com

Neighborhood: Point Loma

SAVOR THE FINEST
BREADS AND PASTRIES

Nationally recognized for its European-style breads and pastries, the Bread & Cie Company was one of the first artisan bakeries established in San Diego. Using age-old artisan techniques, breads are created with all-natural ingredients and baked in a ten-thousand-ton, stone-hearth oven imported from Europe. Step into the café, order a cappuccino, and choose from the very best selection of handmade breads and pastries baked daily plus a variety of sandwiches, salads, and breakfast fare. Old-world country bread favorites include Seedy Sourdough, Fig and Anise, Black Olive, and Raisin Walnut. Guests never mind waiting in line to get a taste of the delicious croissants, Danish, muffins, cinnamon rolls, turnovers, scones, French macarons, biscotti, madeleines, napoleons, and cream puffs.

350 University Ave., San Diego, 619-683-9322
breadandcie.com

Neighborhood: North Park

HAVE CHICKEN PIE
AT A HILLCREST ICON

Step into a legendary eatery that's been serving the hungry public since 1938. The Chicken Pie Shop hasn't changed the menu or recipes since the beginning, making this destination a step back in time. Just as the name implies, most patrons are ordering a meal that includes chicken made the old-fashioned way. All their meals are prepared fresh daily, using quality ingredients and tried-and-true preparations that result in lines out the door from morning to night. Who can resist a chicken pie or fried chicken dinner with several sides and a slice of fresh fruit pie for under $10? With memorabilia adorning the walls and waitstaff buzzing between tables, it will take you back to a simpler time in America.

2633 El Cajon Blvd., San Diego, 619-295-0156
sdpieshop.menutoeat.com

Neighborhood: Hillcrest

SIP ON A SPECIAL ROAST
AT CAFFE CALABRIA

If you are an avid coffee lover, be sure to join the crowds at Caffe Calabria for a special roast from the finest beans in the world. With all expert roasting performed on-site, the quality and selection is unmatched, and professional baristas are ready to create a cup with aromas that are sure to make you smile. Mornings are buzzing with sounds from the espresso machines, milk steamers, and plenty of conversations as patrons start their day with an eye-opening beverage. But before you savor that first sip, take a moment to appreciate the Barista's milk texturing, which is a technique that creates art on the top of your cup. All of their beans are also available packaged by the pound for home brewing.

3933 30th St., San Diego, 619-291-1759
caffecalabria.com

Neighborhood: North Park

GORGE ON THE BEST
PIZZA AND CRAFT BEER ALL UNDER ONE ROOF

What started as a small pizza joint for locals has become a craft-brewing dynasty in Southern California. This is a success story about two siblings who had a dream of owning a small business and serving simple food in a nondescript storefront in Solana Beach. So why not also offer some of their unique home brews to complement the menu? Fast-forward to today, and this simple idea has blossomed into a company with five locations and the prestigious honor of winning the Great American Beer Festival's "Small Brewpub of the Year" more than once. A visit to the original Pizza Port gives you a peek into the humble beginnings of this local icon, with the same pizza and chicken wings that keep lines out the door.

135 N. Hwy 101, Solana Beach, 858-481-7332
pizzaport.com

Neighborhood: Many locations throughout San Diego

HAVE A TWISTED
FARM FOOD EXPERIENCE

To visit the famous Hash House A-Go-Go, you must bring two things: a lot of patience to wait in line for a table and a very healthy appetite. With every menu item served on gigantic platters, you're guaranteed to stay full for days! A signature dish that will wow your eyes as well as taste buds is the Big O' Sage Fried Chicken & Waffle Tower with two succulent chicken breasts stacked on top of a thick smoked bacon waffle, served with two eggs and plenty of hot maple syrup. Pair that dish with a BLT Bloody Mary and you'll understand why regular patrons are hooked for life. Their reputation is spreading, as several locations are now open across the country, including Nevada, Florida, Connecticut, and Illinois.

3628 5th Ave., San Diego, 619-298-4646
hashhouseagogo.com

Neighborhood: Hillcrest

HOBNOB
OVER GREAT AMERICAN FOOD

Now in its 70th year, Hob Nob Hill Restaurant & Bakery has been serving classical American dishes to generations of patrons. To have this staying power in an industry where change is constant, you can bet that their food and hospitality are unmatched. Most of the offerings are family recipes that remain true to their history. Whether it's breakfast, lunch, or dinner, expect to find all-time favorites throughout the extensive menu. You'll also get something rarely seen these days: every dinner comes with your choice of soup or salad, potato, and vegetable. But this establishment is more than just a great restaurant; it is a cornerstone of this community and the meeting place for regulars that have enjoyed food and conversations together for decades.

2271 1st Ave., San Diego, 619-239-8176
hobnobhill.com

Neighborhood: North Park

MUSIC AND ENTERTAINMENT

LEND AN EAR
AT THE SAN DIEGO SYMPHONY

The San Diego Symphony provides year-round entertainment to many loyal fans. With their first concert played back in the early 1900s, the Symphony has grown into one of the more popular entertainment choices in the city. Performing over a hundred concerts each season, the offerings span classical masters to contemporary as well as a special outdoor concert series between July and September. Both national and internationally acclaimed artists will appear regularly to join the Symphony in joint performances. But it is a special treat to enjoy the music in historic Copley Symphony Hall, a building first occupied in 1929 as a high-end movie theater. Much of the same architecture is visible throughout the building's interior and exterior, adding a nostalgic ambiance to your experience.

750 B St, San Diego, 619-235-0804
sandiegosymphony.org

Neighborhood: Downtown San Diego

REMEMBER
SONGWRITER JIM CROCE

Ingrid Croce keeps Jim Croce's music and memory alive at Croce's Park West in Banker's Hill, providing patrons with a delectably inviting urban experience synchronized with live music. Within the restaurant are distinctive areas for diners, with the main dining room serving as a focal point, and offering a more intimate setting for guests who want to converse in plush and stylish platform booths. An interactive bar offers live music daily, and a generous patio has an extended cabana-style awning that opens into a barroom, dominated by a long 1930s wooden bar for happy hour specials, cocktails, eighteen draft beers, bar snacks, and full dining. The Expatriate Room is separated from the front of the restaurant by a paned glass partition and provides a special venue for musicians to express their passion and independence.

2760 5th Ave., San Diego, 619-233-4355
crocesparkwest.com

Neighborhood: Banker's Hill

LIFT YOUR SPIRITS
WITH LIVE MUSIC

For over forty years, the Belly Up Tavern has been serving daily live music to North County and beyond. Garnering national and local rave reviews as one of the best music venues on the West Coast, this diminutive location has developed a huge reputation. State-of-the-art acoustics and an endless list of artists from every genre imaginable have secured the Belly Up as a must-see. Shows will frequently sell out, so it is important to check the calendar early and secure your tickets online to guarantee admittance. Many internationally acclaimed artists will be seen making a special appearance throughout the year, likely to relive the intimate days when an audience wasn't packed into a football stadium. A café next door serves California cuisine all day and well into the nightly performances.

143 S Cedros Ave., Solana Beach, 858-481-8140
bellyup.com

Neighborhood: Solana Beach

TUNE IN
UNDER THE STARS AT HUMPHREYS

From April through October every year, Humphreys Concerts by the Bay provides an open-air outdoor venue on Shelter Island, hosting some of the biggest names in music. Presenting a wide range of genres, including rock, jazz, blues, pop, reggae, and classical, there's bound to be a performance that suits your mood. Even better, Humphreys is located right next to San Diego Bay, giving you a backdrop beyond compare. For a special occasion, consider the dinner package, which includes a pre-performance three-course meal and drink at the adjacent restaurant and bar as well as tickets to the show. Packages are also available that include an overnight stay in the hotel, giving you a great excuse to let loose without thinking about the commute home!

2241 Shelter Island Drive, San Diego, 619-224-3577
humphreysconcerts.com

Neighborhood: Shelter Island

FEED THE GIRAFFES
AT THE SAN DIEGO ZOO SAFARI PARK

Spanning eighteen hundred acres in rural San Pasqual Valley east of Escondido, the San Diego Zoo Safari Park is home to over three hundred species of animals (many endangered) as well as thousands of plants and flowers. Designed to mimic the free-range natural habitat of nearly all the major continents of the world, the park was also designed as a breeding and species conservation area. Among the many attractions at the park, you'll have the rare opportunity to hand-feed giraffes, get an up-close view of cheetahs speeding up to sixty miles per hour past your vantage point, and ride a jeep through territories frequented by rhinoceroses and other indigent animals. You also have the option to experience a "sleepover" in tents, where the sounds of wild animals surround your campfire!

15500 San Pasqual Valley Rd., Escondido, 760-747-8702
sdzsafaripark.org

Neighborhood: San Pasqual Valley

ESCAPE
TO AN ENCHANTING ISLAND

No visit to San Diego would be complete without a trip to historic Coronado Island. Widely known for the landmark Del Coronado Hotel built in 1888, it is most frequently accessed from San Diego by the two-mile long arching Coronado Bridge stretching over the sparkling water. There is also a longer route by land via an isthmus connected from Imperial Beach. Another option for those interested in a more relaxed and scenic experience is the Coronado Ferry, traversing the San Diego Bay every fifteen minutes between the Broadway Pier or Convention Center and Coronado Ferry Landing. The best part of the trip is that a concentration of shopping and dining options are within a short walking distance, all sporting one of the most extraordinary views in the city.

Flagship Cruises & Events
990 N Harbor Drive, San Diego, 800-442-7847
flagshipsd.com

FEEL THE THRILLS AND CHILLS
OF THE MIRAMAR AIR SHOW

Experience the thrill and excitement of military action up-close at the Miramar Air Show, taking place every October at the location where Top Gun became a household word. In a salute to veterans and their families, the Marine Corps Air Station is opened to the public, offering an incredible display of military might. Start your experience walking through the large display of static aircraft and helicopters, including models from early wars to the most modern technical wonders. Then take a seat for the main event featuring the Blue Angels, other military and civilian performers, and up-close flybys that will literally shake your seat.

Marine Corps Air Station Miramar, San Diego, 858-577-1011
miramarairshow.com

Neighborhood: Miramar

TIP
To prepare for an exciting day, be sure to bring a pair
of earplugs and sunscreen.

FROLIC WITH THE DOLPHINS
AND FEED THE SEA LIONS

With over four million visitors per year, SeaWorld San Diego is a must-see destination. This is the original location, founded over fifty years ago by UCLA graduates. They have 190 acres of entertainment and exhibits, including aquariums, animal acts, and even roller-coasters. For a special experience, though, be sure to don your wetsuit and take a dip with trained dolphins. Your trainer will lead you through an in-water interaction, where you'll learn to communicate using hand signals as well as feeding and hugging these slippery mammals. Advance reservations are required, and sharing this rare encounter with family or friends is highly encouraged.

500 Sea World Dr., San Diego, 619-226-3901
seaworldparks.com

Neighborhood: Mission Beach

TIP
You can also feed the sea lions by hand at designated times throughout the day. Check the day's schedule early in the morning, and secure an up-close and personal spot at the water's edge.

PRACTICE WHIMSICAL WHALE
WATCHING ON THE PACIFIC

Spend some time in the nearby waters of the Pacific aboard one of many tours that take you alongside the migratory channels of gray whales. Their famous seven-thousand-mile migration brings them from the chilly waters off the Alaskan coast, passing San Diego on their way to the mating and birthing grounds of the Baja Peninsula. Interestingly, the first organized whale watching tour began here in San Diego, on top of Point Loma at the Cabrillo National Monument, where thousands of observers packed the hillside in 1950 to enjoy the gentle giants in their natural habitat. A few years later, fishermen began the tradition of escorting passengers on their boats for a closer view, and dozens of charter operations are available from all parts of San Diego today.

Neighborhood: All throughout San Diego

San Diego Whale Watch
1717 Quivira Rd, San Diego, 619-839-0128

Offshore Blue Adventures
Whale and Dolphin Tours
#8, 1500 Quivira Way, San Diego, 310-974-2176

Adventure R.I.B. Rides
1380 Harbor Island Dr, San Diego, 619-808-2822

Next Level Sailing
1492 N Harbor Dr, San Diego, 800-644-3454

Hornblower Cruises & Events
970 N Harbor Dr., San Diego, 800-Onthebay

H&M Landing
2803 Emerson St., San Diego, 619-222-1144

Fun Cat Sailing Catamaran Adventures
955 Harbor Island Dr., San Diego, 619-866-7245

BE A KID AGAIN
AT LEGOLAND CALIFORNIA

Remember those cute little plastic bricks you played with as a kid? Well, now you can experience a whole land full of LEGO creations at the LEGOLAND California theme park. When you enter the park, you can't miss the amazing Bronte, the bright red brontosaurus standing at nine feet tall and thirty-four feet long. There are over sixty rides and attractions, including Explorer Island, Fun Town, Castle Hill, Land of Adventure, Imagination Zone, and Miniland USA, which includes reproductions of seven areas of the United States that can be seen from many places in the Park. In addition, two waterparks are especially enjoyable during the warm San Diego days. With all the fun, you are sure to work up an appetite, and a variety of family-friendly restaurants are available to choose from.

1 Legoland Dr., Carlsbad, 760-918-5346
california.legoland.com

Neighborhood: Carlsbad

TIP
Skip long lines by arriving before noon and starting in the back of the Park.

LOSE YOURSELF
ON A VINTAGE ROLLER-COASTER

Take a thrill ride next to the Pacific Ocean aboard a vintage wooden roller-coaster. First opened on July 4, 1925, riders paid only fifteen cents to enjoy the Giant Dipper, also known as the "Mission Beach Roller Coaster" at Belmont Park. Today, special Day Passes are available to enjoy many of the other park attractions, including several carnival-style rides as well as a climbing wall, zip line, laser tag, arcades, go-carts, bumper cars, and miniature golf. Belmont is also home to a unique form of water sport, where a special indoor wave machine creates an endless opportunity for surfers and body boarders to catch the perfect wave without sitting in the ocean for hours. Perfect for families, friends, and parties of every occasion.

3146 Mission Blvd., San Diego, 858-228-9283
belmontpark.com

Neighborhood: Mission Beach

FLY AWAY
IN A HOT AIR BALLOON

Mild weather patterns throughout the year make San Diego a perfect location for hot air ballooning. With a large concentration of professional balloon companies providing services throughout the area, but mostly in North County near Del Mar, an endless supply is available to meet your desire for thrill seeking. No experience is more exhilarating than floating quietly above the coastal landscape, where you can view mountains, valleys, beach towns and, of course, the ocean. A wonderful activity for any special occasion, most rides include a champagne toast for adults. One of the most popular choices is a sunset sail, where the golden hues of dusk paint the sky and ocean with brilliant colors. Nearby in Temecula, the city hosts a balloon festival every May.

Neighborhood: All throughout San Diego

SPEND THE DAY
AT THE SAN DIEGO COUNTY FAIR

Considered one of the largest fairs of its kind in North America, the San Diego County Fair regularly tops a million and a half visitors every year during its run between early June and the Fourth of July. Originally established as an agricultural fair in 1880, it soon grew to a multifaceted entertainment mecca featuring animal and farm exhibits, local and nationally recognized musical performers, retail and hobby tents, carnival rides, and some of the most calorie-packed food choices imaginable! Be sure to reserve an entire day and evening for your visit to guarantee you have enough time to enjoy everything the whole fair has to offer. Besides, who could resist tasting a deep-fried Twinkie at least once in your life?

2260 Jimmy Durante Blvd., Del Mar, 858-755-1161
sdfair.com

Neighborhood: Del Mar

MEET UP
ON BROADWAY

For a special evening out on the town, make a date to see one of the many nationally recognized theatrical events showcased at Broadway San Diego. Their permanent home is located in the San Diego Civic Theater downtown, with highly acclaimed productions offered throughout the year, including such well-known titles as *Phantom of the Opera*, *The Lion King*, *Annie*, *Beauty & the Beast*, and *Riverdance*. This performing arts center has one of the finest acoustical interiors in Southern California, with a rich history and three-thousand-seat capacity. Regularly selling out during the season, you are bound to experience a special performance from highly talented entertainers. Its central location is also an easy walk from downtown San Diego's best restaurants, many of which offer special preshow dinner packages.

3666 Fourth Avenue, San Diego
broadwaysd.com

Neighborhood: Downtown

SOME PRESHOW RESTAURANTS TO TRY

The Westgate Room
1055 2nd Ave., San Diego, 619-557-3650

The Melting Pot
901 5th Ave., San Diego, 619-234-5554

First Avenue Bar and Grille
(In The Bristol Hotel)
1055 1st Ave., San Diego, 619-232-6141

DON'T MISS
THE SAN DIEGO BAY
WINE AND FOOD FESTIVAL

For several glorious days each November, the Embarcadero Park in downtown San Diego hosts one of the largest festivals of its kind in the nation. Drawing over 10,000 participants each year, the San Diego Bay Wine and Food Festival showcases the talents from over seventy local restaurants and two hundred suppliers of liquid gold, including wine, beer, and spirits. The festival typically spans an entire week, with tickets available for educational wine tastings, celebrity chef dinners, culinary classes, and the Grand Tasting Event, where you have the opportunity to stroll along the waterfront and sample some of the finest culinary offerings in the city. This is your chance to rub shoulders with premier chefs and sommeliers as well as the winemakers and brewmasters of our day.

Embarcadero Marina Park North, San Diego, 858-578-9463
sandiegowineclassic.com

Neighborhood: Downtown

MARDI GRAS MADNESS
"WEST COAST STYLE"

Considered one of the largest Mardi Gras celebrations on the West Coast, the Gaslamp Quarter in downtown San Diego becomes a vibrant party on Fat Tuesday before the Lenten season. The night begins with a parade on 5th Avenue through downtown, complete with colorful floats, flashing lights, and plenty of beaded necklaces. The festival also showcases roving entertainers, including showgirls, acrobatic artists, dancers, and costumed stilt walkers as well as DJs and musical artists from around the world. For a special experience, treat yourself to a VIP ticket, which gains you access to exclusive and private parties for the entire evening. Best of all, the Gaslamp is within walking distance of a large number of excellent hotels for a convenient (and safe) sleepover after the night's festivities.

sdmardigras.com

Neighborhood: Downtown

ROCKIN' AT THE CASBAH

Although plenty of options for listening to live music are available throughout the city, the Casbah is a place that must be experienced. Featuring nightly performances that range from the subtle to the extreme, the Casbah has built a reputation as a must-see experience in the heart of downtown San Diego. Now celebrating its 25th year, this intimate venue has been host to some of the biggest names in the business, including Nirvana, Smashing Pumpkins, and Weezer. But the lines are long nearly every night for many of the up-and-coming acts as well as many of the most popular local groups. Other rooms are available throughout the night offering pool tables, video games, a full bar, and plenty of lively conversation!

2501 Kettner Blvd., San Diego, 619-232-4355
casbahmusic.com

Neighborhood: Downtown San Diego

CRUISIN' TO PARADISE

Are you thinking it would be fun to sail from one spectacular tropical location to another, where everything is included, from a room to twenty-four-hour food service, drink, and entertainment? San Diego is home to a large and newly constructed Cruise Ship Terminal at the B Street Pier, making all local downtown attractions within convenient walking distance. Whether you're stopping by on a short Port-of-Call or using San Diego as the beginning and end of your cruise vacation, many options are available during the season from September through May. Several cruise lines offer itineraries that span from a few days to weeks, with destinations that include Mexico, round-trips to Hawaii or Tahiti, and through the Panama Canal to ports in the Caribbean and Florida.

1140 N Harbor Dr., San Diego, 619-683-8966
portofsandiego.org

Neighborhood: Downtown San Diego

ATTEND
A BAYOU BASH

Every May on or around Mother's Day, the Spanish Landing Park next to Harbor Island is transformed into one of the largest Louisiana-themed festivals on the West Coast. Aptly named "Gator-by-the-Bay," this four-day event is a great excuse to let loose and have some fun. The musical lineup is impressive, spanning genres from blues and jazz to zydeco, country, and everything in between. Dancing is optional but highly encouraged! Another focal point is the authentic Southern cuisine, with Creole and Cajun offerings that are sure to leave your palate burning. But don't forget to dive into the crawfish, po' boys, gumbo, jambalaya, and sweet beignets or bread pudding. Many family-friendly activities can be enjoyed as well as a cultural experience and marketplace with festival merchandise available.

3900 N. Harbor Dr., San Diego, 619-234-8612
sandiegofestival.com

VIEW
A SAILING HOLIDAY SHOWCASE

For two consecutive Sundays in December, San Diego Bay is lit up like a Christmas tree during the San Diego Parade of Lights, where boats of all shapes and sizes follow a parade route beginning at Shelter Island and floating past Harbor Island, the Embarcadero, Seaport Village, and Ferry Landing in Coronado. This forty-year tradition has become synonymous with the holiday season in America's Finest City. For those that prefer dry land, many great locations are available along the route to watch the action. But it is an extraspecial experience to participate on the water, with all kinds of private vessels decorated to the gills. Judges are also in attendance to score each boat based on lighting, music, special effects, and originality, with prizes that are worth the effort.

1220 Rosecrans St., # 414, San Diego, 619-224-2240
sdparadeoflights.org

Neighborhood: Downtown

SPORTS AND RECREATION

SURF'S UP!

San Diego is home to some of the best surfing on the West Coast, with spots perfect for beginners and experts. Although the weather is outstanding year-round, the water never reaches temperatures above the low 70s, so most surfers like to don wetsuits. The most popular spots for advanced or professional surfers are the Trestles (located between the San Diego and Orange County borders), Swami's (located near Encinitas and Cardiff by the Sea), and Black's Beach (near La Jolla and Torrey Pines). You can enjoy surfing at other popular tourist beaches around San Diego County, including Oceanside, Del Mar, Pacific Beach, Mission Beach, and Coronado. It just depends on whether you're interested in trekking down steep cliffs or walking right off a sandy beach into the surf.

Neighborhood: All throughout San Diego

FOOTBALL
AND MONSTER TRUCKS

Whether you're in the mood for watching football, professional soccer, music performances, or monster trucks, San Diego's Qualcomm Stadium has been a fixture in the city since 1967. Now the oldest stadium in the National Football League, Qualcomm is home of the San Diego Chargers and also host of the NCAA football Holiday and Poinsettia Bowls. Located in a city known for its year-round mild weather, it's the perfect multipurpose destination for any outdoor event no matter when you visit. Its central location in the Mission Valley area is a short driving distance from most origins and has convenient public transportation options. Best of all, you don't need a heavy coat and hand warmers to survive any event, even in December!

9449 Friars Rd., San Diego, 619641-3100
sandiego.gov

Neighborhood: Mission Valley

TEE TIME
BY THE OCEAN

Considered one of the most scenic in the world, the Torrey Pines golf course sits on the La Jolla bluffs above the sparkling Pacific Ocean, adjacent to a vast state preserve. The thirty-six-hole paradise was built in 1957 on the site of a U.S. Army installation during World War II. The course was named after an endangered species of pine tree that only grows in selected regions of San Diego and nearby islands. For nearly fifty years, it has been included in the PGA Tour and hosted the U.S. Open in 2008. Although the course is open to the public, it's not easy to be awarded a tee time. Many golf enthusiasts take pleasure in simply walking the scenic course treaded by some of the most famous professionals in golfing history.

11480 Torrey Pines Park Rd., La Jolla, 858-581-7171
sandiego.gov

Neighborhood: La Jolla

INDOOR SOCCER
AT ITS BEST

Considered one of the premier indoor soccer teams in the nation, the San Diego Sockers are a fixture in the Major Arena Soccer League. Founded in 1978, the team survived a five-year hiatus to reemerge as a powerhouse in 2009. Now with fourteen championships under their belt, they also hold the record for the longest winning streak in United States professional soccer history, defeating 48 straight opponents during the 2010–2013 seasons. They have also set numerous attendance records, making them a clear sporting destination during the regular season or playoffs. The indoor stadium rocks during games, as the loyal fans cheer the fast-paced action, so bring your loudest voice or earplugs, and get ready for nonstop action!

sdsockers.com

Neighborhood: Downtown

CHEER
FOR THE SAN DIEGO PADRES

Located in the center of downtown's burgeoning East Village, Petco Park is one of the newest and thoughtfully designed major league ballparks in the nation. A unique aspect of this stadium is the incorporation of a local landmark as part of the left field stands. Originally built in 1909, the Western Metal Supply building was declared a historic landmark in 1978. Its tall brick walls are now a prominent fixture in the left field stands, after a complete renovation to house restaurants, bleachers, the San Diego Padres store, and more. No matter where you choose a seat, you'll have views of San Diego Bay, the downtown skyline, or Balboa Park. With a location convenient from anywhere downtown and directly on the trolley line, this stadium is a must-see.

100 Park Blvd., San Diego, 619-795-5000
sandiego.padres.mlb.com

Neighborhood: Downtown San Diego

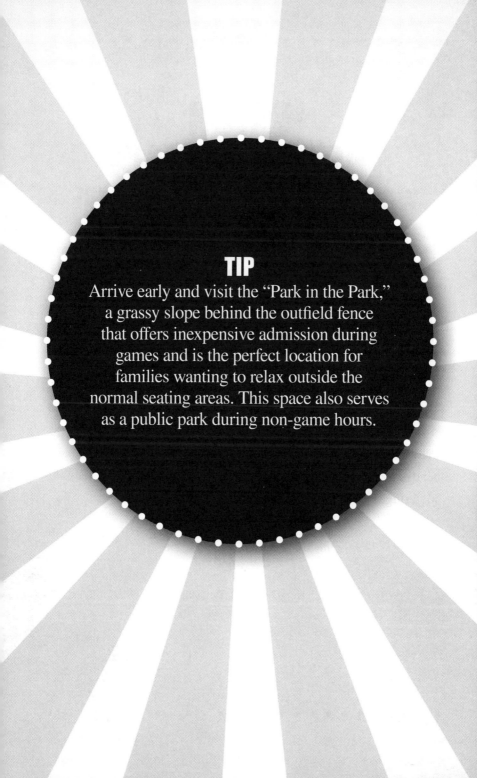

TIP

Arrive early and visit the "Park in the Park," a grassy slope behind the outfield fence that offers inexpensive admission during games and is the perfect location for families wanting to relax outside the normal seating areas. This space also serves as a public park during non-game hours.

WATCH THE HORSES RACE
WHERE THE SURF MEETS THE TURF

Back at the opening of this racetrack in 1937, it was Bing Crosby who crooned the now-famous "Where the Turf Meets the Surf" tune describing the Del Mar icon within walking distance of the blue Pacific Ocean. Every year between July and September and October and November the quiet racetrack is transformed into a heart-pounding match between thoroughbred horses and their jockeys. It is a tradition that is both fun to watch and wager, if you have the nerve! Opening day is especially unique, as all eager spectators are encouraged to slip into their best outfits and wear distinctive hats to mark the start of racing season. Ladies and gents don extraordinary headwear, making the day one of the most notable all year. Satellite wagering is also offered year-round.

Del Mar Racetrack
2260 Jimmy Durante Blvd., Del Mar, 858-755-1167
dmtc.com

Neighborhood: Del Mar

BOOK A STAY
AT AN AWARD-WINNING RESORT

Open since 1989, the Mediterranean-inspired Rancho Valencia Resort & Spa is one of the most sought-after five-star resorts and Southern California's only Relais & Châteaux property. Relais & Châteaux is an association of the world's finest hoteliers, chefs, and restaurateurs that has set the standard for excellence in hospitality. An all-suite property, guests can relax amidst forty-five acres of lush gardens, citrus fruit trees, and olive groves. A rejuvenating Spa and Fitness Center offers tempting choices to soothe the soul with the revitalizing benefits of herbs, flowers, oils, and minerals. And no stay would be complete without an eating adventure at the two distinctive on-site restaurants, The Pony Room and Veladora, which showcase Rancho Valencia's handcrafted cocktails and a farm-to-table philosophy.

5921 Valencia Cir., Rancho Santa Fe, 858-756-1123
ranchovalencia.com

Neighborhood: La Jolla

FEEL LIKE A SEAGULL
FOR A DAY

Situated 320 feet above the ocean atop the bluffs of Torrey Pines is a historical landmark first established in the 1930s that continues to operate as a city-owned, private-use glider port for anyone who thrives on thrilling experiences. No visit to San Diego would be complete without a daring ride on a hang glider, paraglider, or sailplane. Be sure to choose a tandem flight with one of the professional staff members, who are considered some of the most experienced in the world. It is a once-in-a-lifetime experience, as most flights will last twenty to twenty-five minutes, allowing you a true bird's-eye view of the scenic Pacific coast and surrounding landscape. Lessons and certifications are also available for those interested in making the sport a more regular part of their lives.

Torrey Pines Gliderport
2800 Torrey Pines Scenic Drive, La Jolla, 858-452-9858
flytorrey.com

Neighborhood: La Jolla

GET SOME R&R
ON A PRIVATE PENINSULA

Situated on a private fifteen-acre peninsula surrounded by the Pacific Ocean and Coronado Bay, Loews Coronado Bay Resort boasts a stunning view of the San Diego skyline, both day and night. An ideal getaway that combines surf and sun with the casual elegance of an oceanfront home, the rooms take inspiration from Spanish missions and contemporary yachts, integrating an eclectic mix of traditional pieces combined with modern touches. All guest rooms include a private balcony for al fresco dining, and guests can relax by three heated pools or enjoy a spa treatment. The Mistral restaurant serves a global-fusion menu that showcases Mediterranean flavors, tapas-style small plates, and seafood. You're also only a short walk from the Silver Strand State Beach.

4000 Coronado Bay Rd., Coronado, 619-424-4000
loewshotels.com

Neighborhood: Coronado

HOLIDAY
ICE-SKATING BY THE SEA

Built in 1888 and designated a National Historic Landmark in 1977, the Hotel del Coronado never fails to transform itself into a lavish holiday wonderland with spectacular decorations, including a giant Christmas tree in the main lobby and thousands of white lights adorning the historic Victorian building. With regular activities scheduled for guests of all ages, the most unique Southern California experience is their Skating by the Sea event, featuring beachfront ice-skating overlooking the Pacific Ocean. Every year the oceanfront Windsor Lawn is transformed into a spectacular ice rink, with skating sessions offered daily from Thanksgiving through New Year's Day. Complete with holiday music and drinks to warm you up, it's the perfect experience for couples, friends, and family.

1500 Orange Ave., Coronado, 619-435-6611
hoteldel.com

Neighborhood: Coronado

GO SPORT FISHING

Considered one of the birthplaces of modern saltwater sport fishing, our coast has been a fisherman's paradise dating back to the early 1900s. San Diego was known as the "tuna capital of the world," with the largest commercial fishing fleets and canneries anywhere. Today, it is home to a massive sport fishing industry, with charters ranging from half-day to several days or weeks. Whether you're a weekend angler or serious sports fisherman, there's bound to be a perfect option. Although the larger species of tuna and marlin require a lengthier trip, many other smaller fish swim through the kelp beds offshore, including rockfish, bass, halibut, and others. All charters have processing services available, where they'll prepare your fish into convenient fillets and even vacuum-pack, freeze, and ship them to your home.

Neighborhood: All throughout San Diego

RENT A MOTORCYLE
AND CRUISE THE SCENIC HIGHWAYS

There's nothing more exhilarating than touring the San Diego byways on a motorcycle, where you feel one with the road and your surrounding environment. And if that sounds like your kind of thrill, what could be better than cruising on a two-wheeled legend? Renting a Harley is easier than you think, and the local area is packed with perfect day trips in almost every direction. Strap on your helmet, don your best leather garb, and feel the rumbling power of an American-made classic beneath, as you travel along some of Southern California's most scenic highways. Take your pick of routes with sweeping curves through mountains and desert, or follow Highway 101 through legendary coastal towns. For this journey, a beard and tattoos are optional!

Neighborhood: All throughout San Diego

TAKE
A SCENIC BYCYCLE ADVENTURE

The nearly perfect climate in San Diego is a haven for avid bikers, with year-round sunny skies and no rain or snow to challenge your balance. But you don't need to haul a bicycle or two on your car to enjoy the local landscape. Consider renting a bike in the many coastal areas with bike paths that stretch for miles along some of the most scenic routes in San Diego. With over three miles of wide concrete pathways stretching along the ocean from Pacific Beach to Mission Beach, the Oceanfront Boardwalk is a great place to enjoy a day or night meandering among the many walkers, runners, skateboarders, and rollerbladers. Many of the businesses along the route have bike parking areas, so you can take a break and shop or eat while soaking up the beach experience.

Neighborhood: All throughout San Diego

STROLL THE BOARDWALK
IN OCEANSIDE

Spend a day in the third-largest city in San Diego County, strolling along the boardwalk of Oceanside in North County. With a pedestrian path stretching nearly two miles along the Pacific Ocean, numerous activities and attractions are available to keep you busy. A centerpiece is the Oceanside Pier, one of the longest wooden spans on the West Coast and the destination of hundreds of fishermen lining the structure every morning to compete with pelicans and harbor seals for the many species of fish swimming between submerged pillars. Beach volleyball, biking, rollerblading, and surfing are also popular sports available. Be sure to reserve a window seat at one of the restaurants lining the boardwalk, as the sunsets are spectacular year-round.

North Pacific St., Oceanside, 760-435-4500
ci.oceanside.ca.us

Neighborhood: Oceanside

HIKE AMONG
THE ENDANGERED TORREY PINES

San Diego is chock-full of scenic hiking trails, ranging from easy walks perfect for small kids to extremely challenging treks meant for experienced athletes. If you're having trouble deciding which location is best, consider Torrey Pines State Natural Reserve, one of the most popular coastal locations you'll find anywhere in the United States. Six main trails are available to help you traverse the 2,000-acre landscape that once supported the strategic post of Camp Callan during World War II. Beginners should choose the Guy Fleming trail, a level two-thirds-mile loop that will take you through groves of Torrey Pines, sandstone landscapes, and beautiful ocean bluffs. For the more experienced, consider the Beach trail, which winds slowly down through scenic chaparral to a steep descent via steps to the Pacific Ocean.

12600 N Torrey Pines Rd., La Jolla, 858-755-2063
torreypine.org

Neighborhood: La Jolla

DITCH YOUR SWIMSUIT
AT BLACK'S BEACH

This is a destination for those feeling most adventurous! Considered one of the largest "clothing optional" beaches in the United States, Black's Beach stretches for one mile between La Jolla Shores and Torrey Pines State Beach. It is very secluded and difficult to access, making it a popular hangout for nudists and naturists. Named after the original landowner, this city-owned area has only a few entry routes, either along the beach or down steep cliffs from locations near the Torrey Pines Gliderport. But that doesn't deter the many visitors who enjoy a day at the beach wearing nothing but sunscreen! This is also a popular surfing location because of a submerged submarine canyon offshore that creates challenging waves. A word of advice: be extra careful while climbing the steep cliffs, and wear good shoes for the trek.

2800 Torrey Pines Scenic Dr., La Jolla, 858-452-9858

Neighborhood: La Jolla

CLIMB ON TOP
OF POTATO CHIP ROCK

High atop the Mount Woodson hiking trail is a natural rock formation that has become popular with photo enthusiasts posting on Facebook and Instagram. Aptly named Potato Chip Rock, this thin and flat formation is perched in a stunningly beautiful location with endless views of Poway and the Blue Sky Ecological Preserve. Be prepared for the climb and bring plenty of water if it's hot, as the five-mile trail to the top is challenging even for frequent hikers. But the journey is worth the time, as the remainder of your journey is downhill, thankfully! The highlight of your day will be an opportunity to flash a few photos on top of an Internet icon, so bring a friend and some imagination.

Lake Poway Park
14644 Lake Poway Rd., Poway
poway.org

Neighborhood: Poway

INVESTIGATE
THE COASTAL TIDE POOLS

Several beaches in San Diego are prime locations for observing the aquatic ecosystem during low tide. With the regular ebb and flow of the Pacific Ocean, certain coastal locations throughout San Diego become a window into another world, where the receded seawater strands crustaceans and other sea creatures for several hours each day. Tide pools are especially popular with school-aged children, who can learn about aquatic life up-close and also have a lot of fun at the same time. The best locations from north to south include South Cardiff State Beach, Flat Rock south of Torrey Pines State Beach, under the Ocean Beach Pier, and directly below Cabrillo National Monument in Point Loma. Be sure to check the daily tide report, and wear some waterproof footwear!

Neighborhood: coastal locations throughout San Diego

BASK IN THE SUN
WITH SEA LIONS

Although Southern California offers many locations for observing sea lions in controlled habitats, a small area of La Jolla provides a chance to see them up-close in a natural environment. Originally designed as a protected swimming area for children back in the 1930s, the La Jolla Children's Pool has become a resting place for sea lions and Harbor seals as well as a prime location for annual birthing of pups. Although the beach is open to the public, swimming is discouraged, and no one should get too close to these ocean natives. But the proximity allows for spectacular photographs and a window into the lives of these gentle creatures. Just north of the beach is Seal Rock, a small rocky island that hundreds of seals use as a resting place.

850 Coast Blvd., La Jolla, 619-235-1169

Neighborhood: La Jolla

RUN
WITH THE GRUNIONS

Ready for some late-night action at the local beaches? During the spring and summer months, you can witness a natural wonder but only during high tide and nearly always in the middle of the evening when most residents are fast asleep. Grunions are 5–7 inch sardine-like fish, with a spawning ritual that draws crowds of flashlight-bearing humans each year. Thousands can be seen hopping out of the surf to lay eggs in little burrows and returning to the depths. An online resource is available to help you plan the right timing, but it's never guaranteed that the grunions will oblige. If nothing else, you can have a good laugh with other visitors during the nighttime hours and enjoy soothing sounds of the ocean surf.

wildlife.ca.gov

Neighborhood: San Diego beaches

ROAST S'MORES
ON THE BEACH

Next time you plan to spend a day at the beach remember to bring some graham crackers, chocolate bars, and marshmallows because nothing compares with a nighttime ritual that always draws family and friends together. From south of Imperial Beach to the northern borders of Oceanside, San Diego County is home to a great many beaches that allow bonfires, including many with permanent fire rings made of solid stone. You'll need to supply the wood and fuel, so plan ahead. Also, be sure to stake your claim early to guarantee a spot, and don't be shy about sharing the experience with other beachgoers. After all, freshly made S'mores are meant to be enjoyed together, and they actually taste better when consumed in the great outdoors!

Neighborhood: San Diego County beaches

DIVE! DIVE! DIVE!

Well, okay, maybe that phrase is mostly used for submarines, but it's a familiar chant for scuba enthusiasts everywhere. And the coastal waters of San Diego are filled with submerged wonders awaiting discovery. Due to the heavy military presence in Southern California, a large number of seasoned veterans are available for group or private instruction. Regardless of your skill level, many fascinating underwater sites keep you captivated. Most often visited are kelp beds located throughout the area, featuring thirty-foot forests that are home to many of the local fish and mammals. For the more experienced, just a few miles offshore from Mission Beach is Wreck Alley, with a collection of sunken ships that include the *Yukon*, a decommissioned 366-foot Canadian destroyer.

Neighborhood: San Diego coastal waters

PAMPER YOURSELF
AT CAL-A-VIE HEALTH SPA

Tucked away on 450 acres in the Vista valley just north of San Diego lies one of the most exclusive private resorts in the world. Offering a wellness program that is second to none, this health spa only offers three-, four-, or seven-day retreats, where everything is included to provide an experience like no other. Be prepared to bathe in a comprehensive program that includes health, fitness, nutrition, and mind/body treatments that are sure to transport you into a different world. Only thirty-two villas and suites are dotted among the lush landscape, most offering uninterrupted views in a natural habitat. A daily calendar of activities/events offers endless possibilities for treating yourself to something extraordinary. Advance reservations are a necessity, so planning six to twelve months ahead is highly recommended.

29402 Spa Haven Way, Vista, 760-945-2055
cal-a-vie.com

Neighborhood: Vista

ESCAPE
TO RANCHO LA PUERTA

Just a short distance south of San Diego is a thirty-two-hundred-acre Baja health and wellness retreat with international recognition. Rancho La Puerta has greeted guests for over seventy-five years, with an all-inclusive program meant to help you escape from the ordinary. Offering classes and activities, including fitness, mindful wellness, cooking, art, nature hikes, and spa treatments, the daily calendar is bound to keep you busy. Settle into one of the numerous private casitas or villas and get ready to be pampered by an attentive and knowledgeable staff available around the clock. Complimentary ground transportation from the San Diego airport is included for convenience, but it is also an easy drive from many Southern California cities, just across the border in Tecate, Mexico.

5090 Shoreham Pl., San Diego, 800-443-7565
rancholapuerta.com

Neighborhood: Tecate, Mexico

CULTURE AND HISTORY

OFF
TO THE THEATER

Performing Arts are alive and well in San Diego, literally! No matter what your interest, a live theater can be found that will satisfy your artistic side. From classical remakes to original scripts, you're bound to find the right performance throughout the year. The Balboa Theater is a ninety-year old powerhouse in the historic downtown area. Popular Broadway performances are showcased at Broadway San Diego, and the Coronado Playhouse is the longest-running community theater in San Diego. Another much loved favorite is the Cygnet Theater located in the Old Town San Diego State Park. For more theater fun, visit the Lamb's Players Theater, La Jolla Playhouse, North Coast Repertory Theater, Old Globe, Poway Center for the Performing Arts, Spreckels Theater, San Diego Repertory Theater, and the San Diego Civic Theater.

Neighborhood: All throughout San Diego

WALK ABOARD
A FLOATING LEGEND

Proudly moored along Navy Pier in the center of downtown's bustling waterfront, the USS *Midway* is one of the longest-serving aircraft carriers in American history and now a museum worth visiting. You could spend at least half a day walking though the many exhibits and corridors that once housed thousands of navy shipmen and officers spanning forty-seven years from the end of World War II through Korea, Vietnam, and Operation Desert Storm. The tour includes access to sixty exhibits, dozens of restored aircraft, and many interior areas, such as the bridge, galley, and engine room. But nothing is more exhilarating than walking across the massive flight deck with the San Diego skyline and beautiful bay views in the distance.

910 N Harbor Dr., San Diego, 619-544-9600
midway.org

Neighborhood: Downtown

EXPERIENCE
ART ALIVE

For one glorious spring weekend each year, the San Diego Museum of Art is transformed into a living masterpiece that is a must-see for any cultural aficionado. Normally one of the more frequently visited museums in historic Balboa Park, patrons are treated for only a few days to a visually stunning union of paint and plant. Now in its third decade, the Art Alive exhibit is a showcase of over a hundred floral interpretations paired with famous works of art from the Permanent Collection. In addition, the interior rotunda is centerpiece to a two-story sculpture of plants and flowers, perfect for relaxing on a bench and appreciating the creativity of local artists and designers. Your donation will also ensure that the event continues through the years to come.

1450 El Prado, San Diego, 619-232-7931
sdmart.org

Neighborhood: Balboa Park

EXPLORE
THE LA JOLLA SEA CAVES

Carved out of seventy-five-million-year-old sandstone, the seven La Jolla Sea Caves are a wonder to experience. Most of the caves are only accessible by kayak and completely hidden to landgoers, although the large Clam's Cave is a popular photograph opportunity due to its double-sided opening seen from the cliff top. Several convenient kayak rental facilities are located in the La Jolla Shores area, offering individual and group tours to visit these natural wonders. Also be sure to stop by the Sea Cave store on Coast Blvd, which houses a one-hundred-year-old manmade tunnel spiraling down to the Sunny Jim Cave, one of the only sea caves accessible by land on the California coast. Historical artifacts and pictures are also available in the small museum.

1325 Coast Blvd., La Jolla, 858-459-0746
cavestore.com

Neighborhood: La Jolla

DISCOVER
THE CABRILLO NATIONAL MONUMENT

Discover where European expeditions first set foot anywhere on the West Coast of the United States in 1542. The Cabrillo National Monument is a historical landmark situated at the very southern tip of Point Loma and includes an educational center, museum, working lighthouse, and trails leading down to ocean tide pools. Although the park is open year-round, a very popular festival and reenactment of the event is celebrated every October. The site was also a strategic military outlook during wartime, and some of the old artillery batteries are still accessible to visitors. Be sure to mark your visit with a photo including the large statue of Juan Rodríguez Cabrillo, standing at the summit with San Diego and the Pacific Ocean in the distance.

1800 Cabrillo Memorial Dr., San Diego, 619-557-5450
nps.gov

Neighborhood: Point Loma

GET INSPIRED
BY THE LIVING EARTH

Discover what inspires you at the Living Coast Discovery Center, a nonprofit zoo and aquarium situated on the Sweetwater Marsh National Wildlife Refuge on the southern edge of San Diego Bay in Chula Vista. The Discovery Center not only inspires curiosity but also offers a unique opportunity for guests of all ages to explore the living earth. Take part in hands-on exhibits and up-close encounters with more than 350 plant and animal species native to Southern California coastal habitats, including endangered sea turtles, stingrays, leopard sharks, jellies, shorebirds, reptiles, and a large collection of raptors, such as hawks, falcons, owls, an American bald eagle, Golden eagle, and more. Plan a day visit, attend a day camp, make a field trip, or simply volunteer your time.

1000 Gunpowder Point Dr., Chula Vista, 619-409-5900
thelivingcoast.org

Neighborhood: Chula Vista

CELEBRATE
ITALIAN HERITAGE

For one weekend every October, the streets of Little Italy San Diego are transformed into one of the largest Italian festivals in the United States called the Little Italy Festa. With 120,000 visitors packing the streets, you'll get to engage in everything that's Italian, from sampling the cuisine from the best restaurants to taking part in cooking demonstrations scheduled throughout the day. Live music offered on three stages allows you to sing and dance, and you'll also have the opportunity to engage in a friendly game of bocce ball and stickball. One of the most popular attractions is located on the sidewalks below your feet, where professional artists share their talent using Gesso Italiano, a detailed form of art using colored chalk to create images that must be experienced in person.

Little Italy Association
2210 Columbia St., San Diego, 619-233-3898
littleitalysd.com

Neighborhood: Little Italy

TRAVEL BACK
IN TIME

Considered one of the most visited attractions in all of San Diego, strolling through Old Town San Diego State Historic Park is a momentous experience. Registered as a State Landmark in 1969, the twenty-nine-acre village has been restored to highlight life during the first West Coast settlement of Europeans. First established as a military outpost in 1769, it grew to become birthplace of the town of San Diego in 1820. A number of buildings from the early to mid-1800s have been revitalized, including a schoolhouse, blacksmith's shop, newspaper office, and stables. Museums contain furniture and other artifacts most commonly used by these settlers. There are also various stores, where local artisans like to display their talents and expertise. Entry into the state park or any of its museums is free of charge.

4002 Wallace St., San Diego, 619-220-5422
oldtownsandiego.org

Neighborhood: Old Town San Diego

BRUSH SHOULDERS
WITH WORLD-FAMOUS COMIC CREATORS

Once a year, downtown San Diego is altered into a surreal landscape of animation and entertainment. Considered one of the largest premier comic book and popular arts–style conventions in the world, Comic-Con International San Diego draws over one hundred thirty thousand attendees and bystanders. The San Diego Convention Center presents comic books and comic art to a growing audience of enthusiasts, many dressed in outrageous costume attire that puts Halloween to shame. Originally started as a Comic Book Convention in 1970 by a group of San Diegans, the event has transformed into a multimedia sensation including all genres of collectibles, toys, and games. You're also guaranteed to brush shoulders with world-famous comic creators, producers and writers, film and television directors, science fiction and fantasy authors, actors and artists.

San Diego Convention Center
111 W. Harbor Dr., San Diego, 619-491-2475
comic-con.org

Neighborhood: Downtown

TAKE A STROLL
THROUGH THE FLOWER FIELDS

Dating back to the 1950s, a prominent hillside in Carlsbad is home to one of the most spectacular color showcases of the year. Growers from the Carlsbad Ranch spend months preparing The Flower Fields at Carlsbad Ranch with a meticulously planned palette, filling the fifty-acre space with thousands of Giant Tecolote Ranunculus flowers. A member of the buttercup family, this colorful flower blooms for several weeks from March to May. Visitors flock to the fields every year, taking the opportunity to walk along the vibrant landscape, which includes a large portrait of the American flag. Freshly cut bouquets are available for purchase, and the remainder of the crop is used to harvest bulbs for sale or replanting the following year. There is also plenty of space for a picnic or shopping nearby.

5704 Paseo Del Norte, Carlsbad, 760-431-0352
theflowerfields.com

Neighborhood: Carlsbad

INTELLECTUALLY
REWARD YOURSELF

The modern and technologically-savvy Central Library stands nine stories high and features a prominent lattice dome marking the San Diego skyline. Inside, the architecture and interior design boasts mountain and bay views together with many striking features, including a distinctive glass walkway and a charmi ng reading room below the iconic dome. Browse the music and rare book collections or enjoy a leisurely stroll through the Garden Courtyard. Optional tours include exploring the 150 individual pieces installed by the Commission for Arts and Culture, the largest display ever in the history of the Commission, as well as guided tours through the Dr. Seuss-themed Sanford Children's Library or the Society for American Baseball Research Center. Rotating exhibitions can be enjoyed in the fine art gallery and Valeiras Sculpture Garden on the ninth floor.

330 Park Blvd., San Diego, 619-236-5800
sandiegolibrary.org

Neighborhood: East Village

TIP

The Central Library underground parking
offers the first two hours free with validation
for library users. Validation is available
in the 1st floor lobby.

EXPERIENCE THE SIGHT AND SCENT
OF A DESERT BLOOM

For several weeks every spring, the Anza-Borrego Desert State Park is transformed into a landscape of color and fragrance, as the annual wildflowers bloom for a short but spectacular display. This vast state park is the largest in the forty-eight contiguous states, sprawling over six hundred thousand acres in an area just a short driving distance east of San Diego. Although the quality and quantity of desert flowers depends on winter conditions and level of rainfall, you can always count on a beautiful exhibition of wildflowers and cactus blooms that fill the air with a wonderful perfume and provide endless opportunities to take a picture that will impress. This area is also a perfect location for evening stargazing, where light from buildings and streets is at a minimum.

200 Palm Canyon Dr., Borrego Springs, 760-767-5311
parks.ca.gov

Neighborhood: East San Diego County

CAMP
NEAR A FAMOUS OBSERVATORY

One of the premier camping sites in San Diego County is located five thousand feet above sea level in Palomar Mountain State Park. The elevation keeps summer temperatures moderate in the day and cool at night, making it a perfect overnight destination for avid hikers and causal tourists alike. Many of the available trails wind through dense forests of cedar, fir, and pine and open to gorgeous vistas and wide-open meadows. During your stay, be sure to visit the Palomar Observatory, where you can learn about world-leading astronomical research led by scientists from the California Institute of Technology. Three active telescopes are housed in the dome, including the massive two-hundred-inch Hale Telescope, which is the centerpiece of a daily tour for visitors.

19952 State Park Rd., Palomar Mountain, 760-742-3462
parks.ca.gov

Neighborhood: Palomar Mountain

ENTER
A WONDROUS MARINE WORLD

Perched on a bluff overlooking the Pacific Ocean, the Birch Aquarium at the world-renowned Scripps Institution of Oceanography at UC San Diego invites visitors to discover an astonishing array of sea life from the chilly waters of the Pacific Northwest to the warmer tropical waters of Mexico and the Caribbean. View fishes and invertebrates from more than sixty habitats, including more than a dozen seahorse species and their kin as well as pipefish and sea dragons. Other fascinating exhibits include the Hall of Fishes, Coral Displays, and Living Tide Pools. Participate in educational, hands-on activities and plan your next visit around one of the scheduled feedings, which will provide you with opportunities to ask questions and learn more about the natural wonders of the ocean waters.

2300 Expedition Way, La Jolla, 858-534-3474
aquarium.ucsd.edu

Neighborhood: La Jolla

TIP

Parking is free for three hours.

TAKE A
SOUTH OF THE BORDER ROAD TRIP

Just a short thirty-minute drive south of downtown San Diego is one of the world's busiest border crossings in San Ysidro, where you are within walking distance of Tijuana, Mexico. Although visitors are always welcome to drive into Mexico, a much easier choice is utilizing the San Diego trolley and walking a short distance to the many shops and restaurants nearest the border. Once inside, you'll find an endless line of souvenir and trinket shops as well as authentic restaurants serving local cuisine. Street tacos are a specialty of the area, with options for carne asada, chicken, beef, or fish as the main ingredient. Local beer is also a popular draw, with many bars and clubs for late-night entertainment. Just beware that the crossing time back into the U.S. can be lengthy during peak hours, so plan accordingly.

Neighborhood: Baja California

MEET A GHOST
(OR TWO)

A common rumor for generations is that the Grande Colonial La Jolla is haunted. Guests and staff have reported encounters with ghosts in the hallways, stairwells, guest rooms, and kitchen, but no one can know for sure. There's a private room in the hotel with a secluded entry that's popular with guests seeking a quiet refuge. The staff can't understand the reason there are phone calls coming from this room late at night when it's unoccupied. Could it be the spirit of Groucho Marx returning for a visit? As a regular guest, he would stay up late and convince the night staff to play along with him when he wanted to be mischievous. The good news is that all the paranormal sightings are always about people having fun!

Grande Colonial La Jolla
910 Prospect St., La Jolla, 855-267-4884
thegrandecolonial.com

Neighborhood: La Jolla

SPEND THE NIGHT
ABOARD THE WORLD'S OLDEST
ACTIVE SAILING SHIP

One of the landmark ships home-ported at the Maritime Museum, the *Star of India* (originally named *Euterpe*) was born on the stocks at Ramsey Shipyard in the Isle of Man in 1863 and is now located within the Port of the San Diego tidelands. Although you will never actually leave the dock, you will be educated and thoroughly entertained by instructors decked out in costumes and mimicking characters of a bygone nineteenth century sailing era. They will show you areas of the ship that are normally closed to the public and teach you how to move cargo and raise sails. Much like a camping trip, don't expect posh accommodations. The whole purpose of this voyage is to do as the sailors did, and that means sleeping on the 'tween decks (below the upper, open deck) in your sleeping bag.

1492 N Harbor Dr., San Diego, 619-234-9153
sdmaritime.org

Neighborhood: Downtown San Diego's Embarcadero

TIP
Check the website for the exact date of
The Star Of India's Family Overnight.

VISIT
AN EXTRAORDINARY LIBRARY

Named after the longtime San Diego resident and creator of the Dr. Seuss collection of children's books, the Theodor Geisel Library is a unique structure without equal. Situated in the center of the University of California, San Diego campus, this striking building was designed by well-known architect William Pereira, with construction completed in 1970. A prime example of what is called a brutalist/futurist architectural design, the 8-story concrete-and-glass building is a wonder that must be appreciated in person. In addition to the daily use for college students, a permanent collection of approximately 8,500 materials created by Theodor Geisel is stored in a secured location, although a selection is usually on exhibit in the month of March (Geisel's birth month) and over the summer.

9500 Gilman Dr., La Jolla, 858-534-2230
libraries.ucsd.edu

Neighborhood: La Jolla

TAKE A TOUR
OF THE SALK INSTITUTE

Established in the early 1960s by Dr. Jonas Salk, the Salk Institute for Biological Studies has become both a scientific and architectural wonder. Following his development of a vaccine for polio, Salk envisioned establishment of a biological institute to further scientific discovery. In an agreement with the City of San Diego, a total of twenty-seven acres was donated in the La Jolla area overlooking the Pacific Ocean. Under the guidance of world-renowned architect Louis Kahn, the buildings and surrounding area have now been designated a historical landmark. Professional organizations and visitors have appreciated the bold lines and unique uses of natural light for years. Daily tours are available to learn more about the campus, architectural styles, and world-class scientific research continuing today.

Salk Institute
10010 N Torrey Pines Rd., La Jolla, 858-453-4100
salk.edu

Neighborhood: La Jolla

CELEBRATE
LATINO ART

With San Diego's proximity to the border and large Latino population, it's no surprise that the San Diego Latino Film Festival is one of the largest in this country. Although originally established as a showcase for budding students, over the past twenty years it has grown into an event focused on Latino filmmakers as well as feature films, documentaries, and short films related to the Latino community and way of life. Some of the biggest names in the business are in attendance. Tickets can be purchased for single showings, or passes are available that allow you access to nearly one hundred events hosted at theaters and other venues throughout San Diego. Filmmaker workshops are also available for the curious or those considering a career in film.

2921 El Cajon Blvd., San Diego, 619-230-1938
sdlatinofilm.com

Neighborhood: All throughout San Diego

RELIVE
THE EMIGRANT EXPERIENCE

Considered by many as one of the more historic buildings in all of San Diego County, the Warner-Carrillo Ranch House and Museum is worth the 90-minute drive from downtown to experience a piece of history. Open only on the weekends, this ranch house was built in 1857 and served as an important trading post and stagecoach station for travelers entering California from the Overland Emigrant Trail. For many, it was the crossroads for traveling to San Francisco in the north or San Diego/Mexico to the south. Surprisingly, this area in Warner Springs has remained mostly unchanged since the Gold Rush days, giving visitors a sense of life before modern technology. So put those cell phones away and travel back to a simpler time, if only for a few hours!

29181 San Felipe Road, Warner Springs, 619-297-9327
sohosandiego.org

Neighborhood: Warner Springs

GATHER HISTORY
ON THE HIGH SEAS

It's only fitting that one of the most popular museums in San Diego is a collection of floating landmarks! The Maritime Museum of San Diego is located right on the water at the North Embarcadero downtown. Not only do they have the world's most unique collection of historic ships, the museum also has an international reputation for restoration and maintenance. Among the vessels available for touring include the *Berkeley*, one of the first propeller-driven steam ferries on the West Coast, several wartime ships, and two submarines served by the U.S. and Russia. The crown jewel, however, is the *Star of India*. Built in 1863, it is the oldest active sailing ship in the world and a national landmark that also hosts regular educational programs for school-aged children.

1492 N Harbor Dr., San Diego, 619-234-9153
sdmaritime.org

Neighborhood: Downtown San Diego

HONOR THE MILITARY

San Diego has always been known for the strong local military presence, with large stations in the area, including marine bases in Camp Pendleton and Miramar and the naval base in Coronado. Fleet Week was created by local businesses and community leaders and is now running in its eightieth year. This celebration and show of appreciation has become an event that actually spans an entire month and includes many opportunities throughout San Diego to join in the festivities. Events range from an open house and tour at the Naval Air Station, a Celebrity Golf Tournament, and a Classic Car Show to the Miramar Air Show and much more. So bring your American flags, don your patriotic gear, and thank our everyday heroes for their commitment!

5330 Napa Street, San Diego, 619-858-1545
fleetweeksandiego.org

Neighborhood: Downtown San Diego

SHOPPING AND FASHION

SPOT A CELEBRITY
WHILE WINDOW-SHOPPING

Known as the jewel of San Diego, the beautiful seaside village of La Jolla is a shopper's paradise and an ideal place to take a stroll, people watch, and possibly spot a celebrity or two. Walk within one of San Diego's premier neighborhoods located between Girard Avenue and Prospect Streets, where you'll find upscale hotels, restaurants, and high-end boutique shops offering luxurious brands of clothes, perfume, jewelry, and shoes. Fine art is also a popular draw, especially during select Saturday nights throughout the year, when the boulevard is buzzing with live music, wine, and tasty treats in many of the galleries. Although most shops lean toward the high-end shopper, many other options are also available for the more budget minded.

Neighborhood: La Jolla

VISIT
A LOCALLY FAMOUS BOOKSTORE

Touted by fourth-generation owners as "the oldest continuously family-owned and operated bookstore in the United States," Warwick's has been a mainstay in the ever-changing neighborhood of La Jolla. Although the store has experienced a number of upgrades over the past several decades, their service to the community remains unchanged. In addition to the extensive list of new books, stationery, office supplies, and other gifts for sale, they also host regular events, including author book signings and community gatherings. How often do you get a chance to meet an author in person and discuss their latest novel? In an increasingly electronics-driven world, it's a breath of fresh air to stroll through aisles of interesting titles, knowing that you're also supporting a local icon.

7812 Girard Ave., La Jolla, 858-454-0347
warwicks.com

Neighborhood: La Jolla

SHOP
'TIL YOU DROP

If you're looking for a shopper's paradise, look no further than a 1-mile stretch of land paralleling Interstate 8 along the San Diego River Valley. With nearly three million total square feet of retail space, these two expansive outdoor malls include around 250 stores and fifteen anchor tenants. Built over a decade in the 1960s, several expansions and upgrades have created a magnet for both upscale and budget-minded visitors. In addition to the highly recognizable names of the business, many independent and specialty stores are scattered throughout the area. You can easily spend an entire day strolling through the many tree-lined walkways, with a long list of restaurants nearby and also two large movie theaters with a total of thirty-eight screens.

Mission Valley: 1640 Camino Del Rio N., San Diego, 619-296-6375

Fashion Valley: 7007 Friars Rd., San Diego, 619-688-9113
westfield.com

Neighborhood: Mission Valley

NOTHING BEATS
AN OUTDOOR MALL

Westfield UTC (formerly known as University Towne Centre) is a large outdoor mall that epitomizes California living. With over 150 stores and services available, it has become a centerpiece of shopping pleasure in the La Jolla area. Anchor stores include Macy's, Nordstrom, Forever 21, and Sears. Recent renovations have created open spaces with lush landscaping, lounge areas that feature cushioned chairs, and shady spots with Wi-Fi. When you get tired of shopping, be sure to visit the indoor/outdoor Dining Terrace, where you have the unique opportunity to enjoy your meal while watching ice-skaters circle the indoor rink below. The mall is also home to a multilevel 24-Hour Fitness facility and massive ArcLight Cinema with fourteen screens and stadium-style seating.

4545 La Jolla Village Drive, San Diego, 858-546-8858
westfield.com

Neighborhood: La Jolla

FEEL THE HEAT
OF THE GASLAMP QUARTER

The Gaslamp Quarter is a historical district located in downtown San Diego spanning over sixteen blocks from Broadway to Harbor Drive and from 4th to 6th avenues. Step back in time to visit some of the ninety-four historic buildings, most of which were constructed in the Victorian Era. If you love to shop, begin at Horton Plaza, where you can take part in outdoor window-shopping through fashionable stores and art galleries. During the day, many restaurants located throughout the Gaslamp Quarter offer rooftop and patio dining and even opportunities to sip craft cocktails poolside. For those drawn to the nightlife, endless options of restaurants are available to choose from, many with live entertainment, as well as elite nightclubs offering drinks and dancing into the wee hours.

324 Horton Plaza, San Diego, 619-239-8180
westfield.com/hortonplaza

Neighborhood: Downtown

TIP
Park your car at Horton Plaza,
where you'll get three hours of
free parking with validation.

REDESIGN YOURSELF
ON CEDROS

The Cedros Avenue Design District, located in the Solana Beach neighborhood of San Diego, consists of over eighty-five unique shops, art galleries, and boutiques within just two and a half blocks. Many of the items you discover here will be one-of-a-kind and unique pieces for all parts of your home. Whether you're searching for that special wall decoration, handmade furniture, jewelry, linens or lamps, this quaint stretch is a perfect location to stroll and dine without the stress of crowds and noisy automobiles to squash the mood. Treat yourself to many of the health and wellness options, from beauty salons to Pilates to yoga. You also have many excellent dining and drinking options, all within walking distance. Also be sure to visit the Farmers Market every Sunday.

410 S Cedros Ave., Solana Beach, 858-755-0444
cedrosavenue.com

Neighborhood: Solana Beach

SCORE BIG
AT AN OUTLET PARADISE

Get your shopping fix at one of the larger outlet centers just north of San Diego in the coastal city of Carlsbad. Conveniently located right off the Interstate 5 freeway, this center boasts ninety outlet stores, with big names ranging from Calvin Klein, Crate and Barrel, Polo Ralph Lauren, Tommy Hilfiger, and Coach to Jones New York, Ann Taylor, and more. The value of shopping at outlet stores is well recognized, and many tenants offer year-round savings on some of the most exclusive merchandise available. Does shopping make you hungry? A variety of culinary options within or adjacent to the mall offer a wide range of cuisine to fuel you for the day. Also within walking distance are a number of moderate to high-end resort accommodations as well as Legoland California.

5620 Paseo Del Norte, Carlsbad, 760-804-9000
premiumoutlets.com

Neighborhood: Carlsbad

SUGGESTED
ITINERARIES

TEMPT YOUR TASTE BUDS

FAMILY-FRIENDY DESTINATIONS

GIRL POWER

LIQUID LIBATIONS

ACTIVITIES
BY SEASON

SPRING

SUMMER

FALL

WINTER

ACTIVITIES
BY NEIGHBORHOOD

CITYWIDE

DOWNTOWN

ESCONDIDO, EAST COUNTY

LA JOLLA

LITTLE ITALY

NORTH PARK, BANKERS HILL, HILLCREST

MISSION VALLEY, CLAIREMONT, MIRA MESA

ROAD TRIPS

SOUTH COUNTY

INDEX